More Praise for *Ordinary Villains*

"*Ordinary Villains* is the stunning debut collection by E.K. Keith. Welcome to E.K.'s America: you might recognize it. It is an America that is poisoning itself; an America that is forcing young girls to hate their bodies; an America at war with itself and others; an America that believes in a dream that has become a nightmare for most. Many of these poems are rough in their language but sound vaguely familiar. Why? Because they have the ring of truth about them, a sound that is recognizable anywhere and by anyone.

In the world of *Ordinary Villains*, a married man curses at his date at the bar, another man kills himself with heroin and tortures his family, a girl tortures herself to be attractive and everyone follows the American dream—drunk—burning fossil fuel up and down the highways.

These are musical but plain-speaking poems that concern themselves with ordinary lives as they are being lived in the 21st century and are peopled with ordinary, flawed sinners: people like you and me. These pieces are chanted like spells and they weave their magic on the reader: once you read them you will never forget them."

– Natasha Dennerstein, author of *Seahorse*,
Anatomize, *Triptych Caliform*,
and *About a Girl*

Ordinary Villains

E. K. Keith

Nomadic Press
2018

Text copyright © 2018 by E. K. Keith
Cover and spot illustrations copyright © 2018 by Arthur Johnstone
Author portrait © 2018 by Arthur Johnstone

All rights reserved. No part of this book may be reproduced or transmitted in any form or by any means, electronic or mechanical, without written permission from the publisher.

This book was made possible by a loving community of family and friends, old and new.

Requests for permission to make copies of any part of the work should be sent to info@nomadicpress.org.

For author questions or to book a reading at your school, bookstore, or alternative establishment, please send an email to info@nomadicpress.org.

Published by Nomadic Press, 2926 Foothill Boulevard, Oakland, California, 94601
www.nomadicpress.org

First Edition
First Printing

Printed in the United States

Library of Congress Cataloging-in-Publication Data

Keith, E. K., 1969 –
Ordinary Villains / written by E. K. Keith; illustrated by Arthur Johnstone
p. cm.
Summary: The world is full of good people who do bad things—drunk drivers, dumpster divers, absent lovers, astronauts, waitstaff, aunts and uncles, and people who have cell phones. Is that you? If you've ever secretly enjoyed the effects of climate change or thrown away your recycling—even though you worry about the future—you might find a funhouse mirror in *Ordinary Villains*.
[1. POETRY / Subjects & Themes / Politics; 2. POETRY / Subjects & Themes / Love; 3. POETRY / American / General.] I. Title.

2018958533

ISBN: 978-1-7323340-8-3

The illustrations in this book were created using gouache and ink on Canson paper.
The type was set in Garamond Premier Pro.
Printed and bound in the United States
Typesetting and book design by J. K. Fowler
Edited by Natasha Dennerstein and J. K. Fowler

All my love poems are about war

and

all my war poems are about love

and

all of us are responsible for our past and our future.

CONTENTS

LOVE

17 THE GARDEN

18 WORRYING ABOUT THE FUTURE

19 MEDITATION

20 CLEAN SHEETS

21 HENRY DAVID THOREAU'S MOTHER DID HIS LAUNDRY THE WHOLE TIME HE WAS AT WALDEN POND

22 FOR THE LOVE OF XANTHIPPE

24 MYTHIC ARCADE

25 WHAT ARE YOU?

26 FAMILY MYTHOLOGY

27 SIBLINGS

28 RED ENVELOPE

29 JUNKIE UNCLE

30 THANKSGIVING

32 FAST FORWARD NOW AND REWIND LATER

34 OPEN EVERY DAY

36 THE STORY OF THE WORLD

38 ABSINTHE

40	SELFIE
41	EVERYBODY WANTS A LOVER
42	DRIVE

WAR

44	CHALLENGER—JANUARY 28, 1986
46	PAY ATTENTION
47	IT TAKES MORE THAN COFFEE TO WAKE UP
48	FUTURE PERFECT
50	I LEARNED ALL MY SPANISH IN SCHOOL
52	ADVICE
54	DATING POETS
55	UNINSPIRED
56	TELECOMMUNICATIONS
57	SCIENCE FICTION
58	MY NAVEL IS A FUNHOUSE MIRROR
60	APRIL 12
61	BOMBED
62	O SAY, CAN YOU SEE
63	THE DESERT
64	MONKEY IN A DEATHBOX

66	LULLABY
67	IN DEFENSE OF WINSTON SMITH
68	THE KIDS ALL KNOW
70	THE TOOTHPASTE
71	POP QUIZ
72	NARCISSISM
73	TRUE LOVE
75	TODAY'S RELIGION IS TOMORROW'S MYTHOLOGY
76	PROSELYTIZE

RESPONSIBILITIES

77	IDENTITY
79	S.N.A.F.U.
81	SPINDLETOP
82	APPLES
83	WHITE PRIVILEGE
84	PRECIOUS CHILD
85	THE HATE U GIVE LITTLE INFANTS FUCKS EVERYBODY
86	CRYBABY
87	TOOLS
88	THE JUNKY ELECTRIC
89	AMERICA GOES TO A FRAT PARTY

91	MASS INCARCERATION
92	CLIMATE CHANGE
93	DUMPSTER DIVE
94	THE ARCHIVE OF THE EVENING NEWS
95	AMERICA DRIVES DRUNK
97	PENT-UP RESPONSIBILITIES
102	ONE SUPERHERO WON'T BE ENOUGH

ACKNOWLEDGEMENTS

THE GARDEN
for Parry

Sunshine,
the flowers
have all
spread
their petals
in the heat
waiting for
hummingbirds
to come.
Even the bees
sound louder
in the sun,
the sound of flowers
making love.
Waiting for
bees for
hummingbirds
to come,
the flowers
have all filled
with nectar
floating their
thick perfume
up to the nostrils of the sun.

WORRYING ABOUT THE FUTURE

In an infinitely expanding universe   e v e r y b e l l y b u t t o n
is the point of dead reckoning   as we drift as we shift
towards the future while we look at the stilltwinkling lights
of longdead stars   I stop worrying
in a twinkling   The overlap
of the future and the past is the present

Our   hands   touch

I'm worrying   again
because the past failed   to prepare me
for the present   and I'd give anything
for a time machine with anti-lock brakes
to keep us from crashing into the future   like a drunk
on a joyride on a moonless night no headlights
car crumpling fenders buckling
the smack   the impact
I swear I don't know
what happened
and I   never
saw   it
coming

MEDITATION

My navel
gazes back at me
and gurgles
"*I seeeee yooou.*"

CLEAN SHEETS

Love is clean sheets
as a surprise
slide in.

We don't seem
to be able
to keep them clean
for long.

Thanks for doing
laundry
my love.

HENRY DAVID THOREAU'S MOTHER DID HIS LAUNDRY THE WHOLE TIME HE WAS AT WALDEN POND

Transcendentalism is easier
when your mother
does your laundry.

It frees up
your mind
and your time
to ponder
the path of an ant
or make arcane calculations
about the cost of living
at Walden Pond.

Mrs. Thoreau's hands
must have gotten tired
of scrubbing a philosopher's underwear
and pressing the shirts
of a self-reliant thinker.

She   must   have encouraged
his civil disobedience.
A night in jail
would've been her only day off.

FOR THE LOVE OF XANTHIPPE

Pull your head out
of that cave
my darling, Socrates.

There is more
to the world
than shadows
no one can see
playing
on the inside of
your mind.

You are the father
of my sons
but you are
full   of   shit.

Apologize.

Don't make me
dump this chamber pot
on your head.
Don't talk about me
like   I'm   the difficult one.

Who keeps your
house warm?
Who keeps your
belly full?
Who endures the
endless postulations
about
what the world is
how we know it

and what it
all means?

The world is smaller
than we think
and it shrinks
with every new person
who we meet
and what it all means
to a philosopher's wife
is
that any woman
who can put up
with you
will be remembered
as a shrew.

MYTHIC ARCADE

When I was a kid in Texas
California was nothing but a dream,
not much more than a metaphor,
a fantasy of golden glitz and the big screen.

I bet you know a lot about Texas.
I bet I know what you've seen
Alamo heroes, political zeroes,
ten-gallon hats and oil patch schemes.

You can find surfers in Texas
riding in the oil tanker's wake.
You can find California cowboys
speeding up and down the interstate.

You can't see Texas from the inside.
You can't see the mythic arcade.
Just people, running for the money,
inside California it's the same.

If you need roots, go to Texas,
but if you don't belong where you are,
you might find the right place is California.
Who you want to be is who you are.

WHAT ARE YOU?

I am not Black
but that's almost always the first question
you ask me.

I am the child of people
who have been mixing it up in America
for a couple hundred years or so.
I am everybody
nobody ever wanted to be
Mexican   Irish   Cherokee
to name a few.

This hair looks like it looks
and it is a canvas for people
to paint their prejudices
Ugly hair
Good hair
Why don't you straighten that hair?

What's your next question?

FAMILY MYTHOLOGY

Do I have a family mythology?
Were any of my people
eternal fish
who resurrected themselves
after being cut down
in battle?

I am descended
from left-handed outcasts
of two families.

Nobody invites
the Sinister family
to dinner
because Mr. and Mrs. Sinister
have no friends.

They are always reaching
the wrong direction
with the wrong hand
so they get off on the wrong foot.

They produced too many children
who didn't turn out right either.
Not really ambidextrous
an awkward nonhanded inertia
plagues children of backhanded parents.
These children
aren't right.
They flail and flop.
Words cut them down.

SIBLINGS

Brown sparrows
sift trash from a dump
find treasure
in mounds of rotting food
plastic wrappers   aluminum
cans   rusting toasters   shitty
diapers   hairdryers
headless dolls   sideways
refrigerators without doors.

One brown sparrow
beats its wings in the dirt
kicks
and tangles tighter
in a six-pack plastic noose.

RED ENVELOPE
for Shayna Gee

I never noticed
that beauty mark—
a quiet dove perched
on your cheekbone—
until you told me
how bullies made you cry.

It's easy for a beautiful child to believe a jealous lie.

It's harder to believe
when Beauty marks your face,
it's the mirror who tells the truth.

So keep looking past the lies,
keep looking.
See?
There you are.

JUNKIE UNCLE

My junkie uncle was an artist
whose work never went anywhere,
so he lives with my grandmother
and my aunts take care of them both.

They don't get along, my aunts
so they arrive on different days
to cook and clean,
so my junkie uncle and my grandmother
eat and watch TV.

He occasionally disappears.

And my aunts arrive
crossing days,
crossing each other,
crossing words—
martyrs on the holy cross
of family responsibility.

They poke old wounds
until everybody's hands bleed
and still doubt
that anyone's wounds exist
except their own.

I walk past junkies on the street.
Their sisters and mothers
are cooking and cleaning and eating and watching TV.
They argue whose fault and who's to blame
and worry that this is the last time
the family junkie will disappear.

THANKSGIVING

A dozen turkey vultures
spin a double helix
over Thanksgiving roadkill
on the highway to your mother's house.

She used to cook
the classic American feast—
turkey and dressing, giblet gravy,
green bean casserole, mashed potatoes,
cranberry sauce
and a green salad no one ate
to save room for pumpkin pie
and pecan butterball cookies.

We cower beneath your memories
like a newspaper held up
against a thunderstorm
melting into a discussion
of obesity, diabetes, and dialysis.
A mild heart attack
has put her in the hospital
for the holiday today.

Worry is slung under your eyes
like two hammocks left in the rain.
You keep your tone casual.
You keep your grip locked on the wheel.
You wonder if your teenage son
will see his grandmother alive again.

We pet the cats and wait
for your mother's girlfriend of thirty years
to bring her home from the hospital.

There is nothing simple about family holidays
except the food we eat this year—
baked chicken
green salad
quinoa casserole
stevia-sweetened
cranberry sauce and pumpkin pie.

Just for you
she baked pecan butterball cookies—
a double batch.

FAST FORWARD NOW AND REWIND LATER

I can't see the stage   but I really like your hair
I got x-ray vision   I got time to dance
If ya wanna be with me
then there's gotta be romance
I got decisions
revisions   I got full collision

For those who Fail to dance
there will   be   no reward

Fast forward now and rewind later
What'd ya say?
I said I can't talk dirty on company time
I can't talk dirty on company time   call me later

I'm a pie in the sky lemon meringue lover
and I wish your kisses would linger longer
Fucking you is like getting run over by a truckload of feathers
I'll go now so I can come back later
I wish I could send my love by pigeon

Fast forward now and rewind later
What'd ya say?
I said I can't talk dirty on company time
I can't talk dirty on company time   call me later

Ya tell me what yer thinkin   drinkin
lemondrops   peppermint schnapps
and I listen for some reason
while you talk and talk and talk
Yer philosophy is a sunk ship
and my ideal vacation's not yer ego trip

For those who Fail to dance
there will   be   no reward

Fast forward now and rewind later
What'd ya say?
I said I can't talk dirty on company time
I can't talk dirty on company time
Call me later

OPEN EVERY DAY

The jukebox still plays Van Morrison.
I can't call you because I get no signal at the bar
and even though the Giants are behind, it's still a good night.
They lose. Frank says, "Life is horrible"
and he serves another round.
The choir practices the only parts
of "Hot Town Summer in the City"
that they can collectively recall
and there's gossip about a friend exiled to the Florida Keys.

"I fuckin hate it when she does that,"
A guy complains to his date slamming his phone on the bar
"I'm fuckin sick of my old lady checkin up on me.
She should understand
that I'm gonna fuck who I want."
I wonder who shot the rifle over the bar.
There's a shark mandible on the wall,
bumper stickers on the fridge
from roadside attractions,
driving distractions.
Radio stations' mashup signals cross state lines,
white lines slide down the sideview mirror.

Pretty soon California farmers
will be growing giant radioactive artichokes
the size of basketballs.
I suppose the ambient radiation of cell phones
compared to Fukushima
sets my mind at ease, so I try another call.

I like a loud bar with plenty of politics and religion
up for discussion
as the bottoms of our glasses tip up,
get a cheap drink

leave a fat tip
and drink up.
You're at the 21 Club.

THE STORY OF THE WORLD

We all end up paying
for mistakes of previous generations.

My great great great grandfather
stole this
fair n square
and your great great great grandfather
never stopped being mad.

So a decade   a century   a millennium later
I'm mad   you're mad   and everybody's mad at us
and nobody knows what really happened anymore
except what we've done to each other.

And all of us have always been here
so nobody has anyplace
to Go Back To.
And nobody can pay their parents' debts.
And nobody can clean up our grandparents' mess.

So we build little league fields on superfund sites
live in radioactive cities
Chernobyl Nagasaki Hiroshima Three Mile Island.

While kids play in minefields
a ball of plastic big as Texas grows in the ocean
and tires wash up on the beach.
We hold hands under petrochemical technicolor sunsets
breathe smog   watch tarballs   and trash
and hermit crabs in Coke cans.

The young generation's got guns in their hands.
They say
Love thy neighbor.

They say
The meek shall inherit the earth.

ABSINTHE

The music starts
a slow pulse builds to crescendo
dip and rise.

Our world society
in a manic shift
between doing nothing
and revolution
dip and rise.

A tobacco plug
between lip and gum
stand and spit
over the porchrail.
It's one way to quit
smoking
dip and rise.

It's all part of the dance.
You have to trust your partner
not to drop you on your head
now twist
now spin
together
move as one
dip and rise.

The sun
at dusk
at dawn
dip and rise.

Christ died.
And on the third day

the stone was rolled back.
The tomb was empty
dip and rise.

I have no idea who you are
but I'm giving you
hugs and kisses
anyway
dip and rise.

Cornchips
a bowl of guacamole
a divine crunching toothsome joy
dip and rise.

The music of the ocean
the curve of a wave
we ride
dip and rise.

The Green Fairy
flies out of the bottle
a drunken dip and rise.
Embarrassed by her visibility
she dives under the coffee table.
We won't see her again this evening.

What were we talking about?

SELFIE

See America.

It sees you.

Take lots of pictures.

It takes pictures of you.

We are It.

This is our identity crisis.

We are failing to see
who we are.

Look
who we are

EVERYBODY WANTS A LOVER

So where does love fit
in a world of citizen pornographers?

Our fetish machines make us voyeurs
increase curiosity
decrease modesty.

We all need to know
what everybody's bodies look like.
Professional photographs bore
with plastic alterations to private places
or electronic edits to pixelated faces.

With a touch
built-in breakup regrets
torture exes
whether they're in Texas or Timbuktu.

We shame them by posting tokens
of trust broken.
Such mean exposures
but shame on who?

Our culture of vultures
feasting on the remains
of what used to be love

DRIVE

Drive placidly through the noise and haste.
Drive placidly.
Drive.

It's not a secret that most people
waste a lot of time
and if they were doing something different
they would feel better
and in fact be better people.

So tell your secrets to someone
no one talks to
in the buzz and hum of conversations
overlapping rants
pontifications.
Hide your secrets out loud.

It's the tingle of karma and what seeds we sow.
I am an American
therefore I drive.
I want to do the right thing
but I have retroactive amnesia.
I know what I said when I said it
but now I don't remember anymore.
Time is shortstopping for cigarettes
blow smoke in your face
I gotta go I gotta go I gotta go.
It's gonna be an early night.
Or is it?
Good sense has coagulated.
We're all dehydrated
so the last thing we need is another drink
but that's what's likely to happen.

The city smells like urine.
We endure run of the mill pilsner kisses
love without flipflops
love in a full lotus position
love that just misses masking the horror
of what harvest comes of bones in mass graves.

A crackhead sings too softly to be heard
over boomboxes and traffic passing through.
What can soften the flavor of bad dreams
and reality too bitter to smoke?
How do you write a love song in a time of war?
I might as well be sitting in an ashtray
rolling in the dust of my own exhalations.

Sing me a love song anyway.

CHALLENGER—JANUARY 28, 1986

I watched you all die
with my American history class
on a black and white TV
that Mrs. Whittington kept at school.

We had seen televised rocket launches before
7... 6... We have main engines started
4... 3... 2... 1... And liftoff   liftoff

I was young and mildly bored.
Kids in Houston had seen it all before
just before   the Challenger exploded.
We went silent
watching streams of smoke
fork from the booster rocket.
Even on black and white TV
We knew all 7 of you were dead.

And the TV
replayed your death relentlessly.

One girl in our class started to cry
So the history teacher yelled
and sent my friend to the office.
But she didn't turn off the TV
like she couldn't believe it
until the principal came in
and lectured us until the end of class
about being strong.

I rode the bus home alone.

To avoid any unpleasant feelings
my parents talked relentlessly

about where they were
when Kennedy was assassinated.

PAY ATTENTION

A man I dislike
asks me to reinvent empathy.

Some Einstein says
*You can choose to believe that everything is a miracle
or that nothing is.*

Mother Nature knows well that land animals exist
because of water wishing to be dry.

If you *really* think
all our heroes are dead
you are not really paying attention
to the people who have been resisting
thought control against the crush
of so many parties
so many lines
broadcast for so long
in waves
waves
waves

Bye bye.

IT TAKES MORE THAN COFFEE TO WAKE UP

My breakfast cereal
has a concentration of radiation
that I just can't swallow
and somewhere just past the hollow of my throat
I hold in screams
I told you so I told you so I told you so.

But no one listens to children
not then   not now   not later.

It's not just canaries that have stopped singing.
Like stool pigeons
whistleblowers shudder in the dark.

I can see the future as a bleaker yesterday
that has taken the proper precautions
to prevent tomorrow.

So when your gut starts to ache
there's nothing to take.
It's just your intuition
in conversation with your conscience.

FUTURE PERFECT

I'm restless and unwilling to walk in the rain.
A whole world of worry
I'm a flood plain
soaked   and overflowing with doubts.

A hurricane of questions forms
What will I have done by then?
The future is a trap we trip with our heads
stuck in possibilities.

All that I have failed to do
bears the teethmarks
of questions formed in the future perfect.
Stray bullets and raindrops
disco thumping and car wheels on slick streets
nothing is melting.

The ever real present
makes me tense.

I want to be prepared   to be
bludgeoned by current conditions
by the here & now
by external circumstance   by internal deformity
the nonconformity of cells to healthy patterns
catastrophes   metastases
financial collapse   radiation   bombs
dropping   oil leaking
talking heads talking
NOTHING IS MELTING.

It's sweet to think that what doesn't kill you
makes you stronger
but that's just not true

because we're fighting for our lives all the time
and each thing that tries to kill you   and fails
still breaks you down
bit   by   bit
from outside   from within.
We carry seeds of destruction.
We lose the war   by attrition.

Nothing is melting.
I'm restless   and unwilling
to walk in the rain.

I LEARNED ALL MY SPANISH IN SCHOOL

I never tried to pass for White
but I have been passed
because it's good to be White in America
and Mother knows best
to give a not-quite-white baby
White names that don't explain
such dark eyes and such tight curls.
My name never stopped mean girls hissing
gringa cola prieta and guera and taco
brown on the inside
and not-quite-white on the outside.

You would not believe how White people talk
about Other people when they think you're White.
How it's more polite to say Spanish
instead of Mexican
and the subtle shift in tone
when your Mexican is discovered
your tortillas uncovered.

I never tried to pass for White
but I have been passed
because White people who like me
want to give me the benefit of the doubt
and let me tell you, sister
there's nothing like White Privilege
and my mother knew it.
So when people would ask
"Are you Italian or Greek?"
she would laugh and say
"Good guess!"
It is so disappointing
such dark eyes and such tight curls
fail to fit in

not White, not Mexican.

I have been passed.
I identify as White Trash.
My mother is Mexican
but her family doesn't mind
porque no hay indios en la familia.
And since I learned all my Spanish in school
it was years before I understood.
It's good to be White in America.

ADVICE

When a man tells you
"You are beautiful"
don't believe him
so much
his eyes
are your only mirror.

First
his eyes lie
about the perfect clarity
of your skin
in the morning,
the smooth curve
of your lip, the dip
of your navel
the hollow
between your breasts
where the memory of a kiss
still lingers.

Then
when he hurts you
his eyes lie
about the scars
and blackheads
on your face
your fat, pimpled ass
your big belly
your droopy, lopsided boobs.

After
he hurts you
you will stand alone
in the bathroom

brushing your teeth.
The toothpaste-speckled mirror
will crack
in your eyes.

Don't lose your beauty
in a man's eyes.

Keep it for yourself.

DATING POETS

How many times
will I learn
the same lesson?

Dating poets
is kissing guys who haven't come out yet.

Dating poets
is fucking sensitive-on-the-inside art thugs.

Dating poets
is dancing with drama queens.

And really
they're all the same
like that forlorn birdie
asking steam shovels
Are you my mother?

My grandmother says
of old men
cruisin'
the bridge club scene
"He's lookin for a nurse and a purse"
Nana—it's the same as dating poets.

Maybe that's the fate of poets
not lucky enough
to die young, to linger
at the snack bar
waiting for cards to fold
hoping to find
the right woman
with the right dead husband.

UNINSPIRED

I won't breathe
your air   sweet oxygen
to the brain.

Your inspiration
had an expiration date
like that half empty carton
of half and half
that sat in my fridge
for half as long
as we were together.

You left me cold.
You will never be my muse.

TELECOMMUNICATIONS

It's hard for me that people don't like to talk
as much as they used to.
We're connected   but we're not connecting.

And the more my vision pixelates
the lonelier I feel
but I cultivate the pixel farms.
The pixels grow between us.

Nuclear power to electric wire
airwaves and landlines jammed
glowing screens in our hands
we're connected   but we're not connecting.

Meltdown is the predictable conclusion
to toxic conversations
wasted time
wasted money
wasted people
Red Alert.

What do we do?
I want to see your face.

There is no one more bitter
than a disappointed idealist.
Airwaves and landlines jammed
the pixels grow between us.

We're connected   but we're not connecting
and we do not have the slightest clue what to do.

SCIENCE FICTION

Why do we always expect
the cool parts of science fiction to come true?
>	Flying cars
>	>	and rocket boots
>	>	>	and robots who love to do chores.

Who knew what we'd get
is designer germs   frankenfood   smart phones   smarter bombs
games to encourage sociopathic behavior in children
the Hound from *Fahrenheit 451°*   except it *flies*
inefficient robot lawnmowers
nuclear re-escalation
and more mind control options.
Turns out Big Brother is *voluntary*
>	>	and everybody *loves it*?

Where's my rocket boots?
>	Where's my robot maid?
>	>	And where's my flying car?

My country 'tis of thee
Land of the incarcerated
Home of the sedated and the self-medicated.

The Great Experiment
turned dystopian sometime ago
and we're more like rats than ever.

We didn't get a sci-fi preview
for some of the worst of it
but historical precedent.
Zyklon B was a pesticide too.

So what about those chemtrails
What do you think *those* will do?

MY NAVEL IS A FUNHOUSE MIRROR

I gaze at the crazed glazier's masterpiece
and what I get is more me me me   meme.
A meme in time craves crime.
I bought a dimebag while you were trippin balls.
I don't think I've once   ever   heard you cough.
It's your over the counter vacation
that amuses most who battle the flu.
You hide inside the confines of your skull
but   man   your conversation is incredibly dull.
I'm here outside the walls. What Jericho trumpets call
me   Call me   Call me   Insecurity.
Gauge of success: The number of messages I get.

I'd like to be free from electronics
but it's all that's left of connection here
in Radiation Nation. We're frying crisp like bacon.
It's cell phone towers and Fukushima
those old A-bomb paranoias are passé.
Geiger counter click click click

My crystal skull could tell the future
if it could talk.
Here's a row of empty bottles
Whatcha got?
Not a lotta
Time.
You know you're gonna get lucky tonight
even though you snore.   The more I hear you
                                breathe
the more I r e l a x.

I hope that time is more like an ocean
not a rollercoaster click click click Whoa a a a a
and given certain superpowers I

could move freely through   back forth in around
time. It's so tricky.   Can a spiral path
move only forward   in one direction
or is that two or   back forth in around
or is that three or more more more more more

APRIL 12

The first shot is fired at Fort Sumter.
The orbit of Earth by the first cosmonaut.
The first admission that Fukushima is worse than we thought
an upgrade to a Level 7 nuclear disaster.

I bought cheese from New Zealand
butter from Ireland
yogurt from Greece.
West Coast milk is glowing in the dark
and I only want produce from South America.

I'm not good at math
so I'm still calculating
the half-life of radioactive isotopes
in California artichokes.

I'm struggling not to cry.

BOMBED

Fill a million Dixie cups with gin.
Let's drink white trash martinis.
I'll dip my fingers in the olive jar.
Mickey Flynn's on a binge
and you might think Bonnie's nachos
are ice cream for just a second.

You're high on your birthday again

All experiments in utopia are bound to fail
but for five bucks you can get a souvenir shirt
if you don't mind misspellings.
We have crossed the line
between loyalty   and inertia.
Splitting hairs has the same effect as   splitting atoms
in a polite society.
You can try to piss me off
I'll just smile and nod
push a button
presto
The itinerant dead are on tour
sacredhocking, pawnshopping.
What are we doing while all our symbols burn?
Looking at the moon.

Mickey Flynn's on binge.
Don't say I love you
unless you're staying for a long time
or until after you're long gone.

You're high on your birthday again

O SAY, CAN YOU SEE

They don't bury downwinders in lead-lined caskets,
pine will do.

They didn't save the world
but they knew how to have a blast.
Party until your merit badge turned black.

Like good citizens
they stood in the yard,
cold beer and hotdogs,
burgers on the grill,
watching the rockets red glare
the bombs bursting,
the mushroom clouds,
the most beautiful sunsets you can imagine
somewhere north of Las Vegas.

A yokel naiveté about radiation
and every A-bomb test was the Fourth of July.
A sparsely populated location
ideal for its prevailing easterly winds
to protect the dense population of California.

Years later a tsunami hits Japan.
Prevailing easterly winds
bring California the fallout denied for so long.

Carcinogenic and mutagenic
something wicked this way comes
and I'd thumb a ride somewhere
but there's no place to go
where the wind doesn't blow.

THE DESERT

All my loved ones
are on the road.

They like to party with naked cops in the Nevada desert
except my punk brother
who's on tour with the band.

He just saw God
in Tucson, Arizona.

Turns out God's half Asian, half white
good-looking
and slightly more muscular than you would expect
for a guy his size.

God owns a bar
and he's pretty free with the drinks.

He'll give the whole band a tour
of the sex dungeon.
God likes to watch.
God likes anybody to suck his dick.
God is pansexual and decorates with pictures of himself
fucking famous people.

My brother said he's not surprised
God is a Republican.

MONKEY IN A DEATHBOX

You're a monkey in a deathbox
remember that.

You're a monkey in a deathbox
remember that
                panic attack panic attack
pumping pistons and spinning wheels
propel our velocity.

We're traveling as fast as fossil fuels
can take us   somewhere.
We get lost in neighborhoods
where all the street signs are all the wrong color.
There's no way to get back
to where we were before.
We don't want to get back
to the same lost place
anyway anyway any way will do.

Panic attacks strike randomly   like seizures.

Your faith in your ability to survive the moment   seizes up
with the sudden acceleration of your likelihood of dying
in this automobile
RIGHT NOW.

You're a monkey in a deathbox
remember that.

You're a monkey in a deathbox
remember that time
just after the world tilted up side down
and the car
                      drops

but it's okay we had the top down anyway.
Up side down means seatbelted   ass up
and you can't quite grasp why it's so dark
but that's what happens when the windshield hits the dirt.
We crawl through glass to get out from under the car
                         while the tape decks still spins on battery power
                              I'll see you on the dark side of the moon

No one knows the reason why
today's not the day you're gonna die.
I'm a monkey in a deathbox.
I'm a monkey in a deathbox.

LULLABY

What will it take
to abate the hate?

We are the fat lazy offspring
of pioneers
immigrants
and revolutionaries.

We re-create the problems
that our ancestors resisted
and triumphed over.

We will insure that our offspring
will pioneer
immigrate
and revolt.

Lullaby little baby
I hope you wake up free.

IN DEFENSE OF WINSTON SMITH

You're busted. You know it. You don't fight it.

It's your friends who get to torture you too.

You lie, but you know it's futile. Quit.

Everybody's just got a job to do.

Thoughtcrime is not so easy to control.

The Thought Police know your secret profile.

You resist. You resist with all your soul.

The Thought Police use your secret profile.

They know when you'll break and what will break you

and you do.

       You're a rat. You're a rat too.

Double down, I'm Double Agent Other.

I'll tell you what you want to hear me say.

War is Peace Doublespeak Love Big Brother

Better live to rebel another day.

THE KIDS ALL KNOW

American dreams   and California dreams
and I have a dreams   are insubstantial.

Dreams beaten down by billyclubs
and the kids all know
whose lives matter.

The Greatest Generation sold out
their children and grandchildren
and great grandchildren.
They taught America
the need for keeping up with the Joneses.
As conspicuous consumption
nurtures conspicuous corruption
and the wants of the greedy
trump the needs of the needy,
conspicuous consumption became the norm
in a disposable culture
that risks being thrown away too.

Freedom means choosing
among brand name products
while equality plateaus for women
while queer and notwhite folk
struggle up a slippery slope
while justice calls out that Black Lives Matter
to remind corrupt institutions that cops   are   not
judge   nor jury   nor executioner.

The kids all know the world's in trouble.
Look what we've given them—
a double dose of shit rolls down
a planet drowning in its own trash
incendiary politics   relentless clash

of money versus money
and the rest of us don't matter.

It's easier to tune out
the noise of promises and dreams
through isolation disguised as socialization.

At least you know the lies are real.

It's hard to be young
with a whole life ahead
of things just out of your reach.

No matter how many dreams disappear
when you wake up
reality will shake down
your desire to tune out the noise.
The kids all know there's a pecking order
of whose lives matter less.

But the kids are alright
starting revolutions with their thumbs
starting from the bottom up
unpacking the pecking order
with Black Lives Matter
that brings us back
to the dreams that have been broken
and eyes wide open   the kids
will fix it   a shift past dreams
to a waking life.   The kids are alright.

THE TOOTHPASTE

How much toothpaste
do you have to forcefeed a rat
before it dies?
Fluoride is probably
making me
make bad decisions
but I'm afraid of tooth decay.

So I endure synaptic shutdown
on the advice of my dentist
and the municipal water supply
isn't helping either.

My thoughts   queef   out
at times
in irregular   random intervals.
I make 18 bad decisions
for every good one.
I try to focus
I try to focus
but I can't follow
a thought to its conclusion.

It's like trying to decipher
archaic cursive lettering
and sometimes
I almost see it.
I try to focus
but I worry about tooth decay.

So I brush my teeth.

POP QUIZ

True or False?
The effects of Prussian blue on low doses of radiation are completely unknown.

False.
Prussian blue only treats heavy doses of radioactive cesium.
After low dose exposure, Prussian blue is best
for expressing feelings of futility on canvas.
If consumed, expect a side effect
an irregular heartbeat.
Love has the same effect as eating paint.
No Prussian blue for you.

True or False?
You have to eat all your cesium.

False.
The Chernobyl Cookbook says:
Chop your vegetables into the timeliest pieces.
Soak, and wait
until the cesium dissolves in the water.
Boil everything.
There's the tiniest chance
of dodging raindrops.

True or False?
The Godzilla scenario is in fact an optimistic point of view.

True.
Science fiction assumes any future for me and you.

NARCISSISM

The shadow of the Lorax plays
on the walls of Plato's cave
where Christ was buried
and on the third day
Sisyphus rolled the rock away
and invented religion
to fuel old feuds
with folks who might yet be friends.

The world is small   and getting smaller
an unlikely oasis in space.

I am you.
All the myths are true.
We are all gods at all times
and of course we see ourselves
in every drop of water.

It is us.

TRUE LOVE

Do you have a tattoo?
Who here has pierced ears?
What have you done for love and lost?

Once there was a little known goddess of war.
No one remembers her name
because she was in love with the king of the gods
and he loved her   but she didn't know
he was the secret love
of the goddess of love.
So she asks a jealous friend for advice.

The love goddess snorts and says
To prove your love
cut off your ear and give it to him

So she mutilates her body
to make herself more attractive
to her lover.
And he is so horrified   so disgusted
he turns his face from her kiss.

And the truth is
scars are beautiful.

Secretly we all know
it's our imperfections that attract us to each other.
There is nothing more interesting
than a crooked nose
tooth
finger
toe.

And like a little known goddess of war

we wonder who it will be
who will look at our scars
and love us.

TODAY'S RELIGION IS TOMORROW'S MYTHOLOGY

As millennia pass
gods fall out of fashion
and retire to the Florida Keys
where the waves
hush the fading prayers
of the penitent
and the petitioners,
where the old gods watch
the birds swirl, and even condos
have pink flamingos paid in full.

Young gods don't come around much
but people   never   tire
of waiting for messiahs
and emanations
are really just human desires.
The second coming is a story
to keep our hands busy
and the word of the prophet
gets twisted to make more money.
And people   never   tire
of proving their gods' strength.

So the prayers of the penitent
and the petitioner's wails
soak the bloody earth
as we wage war
in the names of indifferent gods
who sip worship like a tropical cocktail.

PROSELYTIZE

Outraged
by noses that aren't small or straight
by hair that doesn't lay flat
by faces whose features refuse to conform
to a common standard of beauty,
they tell us we are ugly.

To defend their common features
they sell us funhouse reflections,
so we don't know what we look like.

I want to convert you
to the religion
of your own outrageous beauty.

I'll build you a church of mirrors
and fill it
with gods like us
whose faces don't match.

IDENTITY
for Jeff Chang

America's a trickster
shapeshifter
doppelganger
ventriloquist.

Perception might be a deception
but then again
maybe not.

I am not
who you think I am
and I know
you wouldn't have said what you just said
if you'd have known I was
that.

We don't know
who we are
or who we have
inside us   no guidance
from our family who survived
tricksters   shapeshifters   doppelgangers
and ventriloquists.

Passing is survival
and mothers will lie
to protect their children.
And if you can camouflage
your child in skin privilege
you will.
You will close your eyes   child
and wake up White.
A sleeper unaware
You're American!

A trickster scheming
shapeshifter passing
doppelganger matching
ventriloquist echoing
the dream
that conceals who we are
the dream
that reveals our society.

We are not yet
who we claim
to be.

S. N. A. F. U.

As Neil Armstrong wiggles into his spacesuit
he breaks the switch that starts the engine of the Eagle.
That happens between
The Eagle has landed
and
One small step for man

I remember a time before you could see
the layer of brown air that floats
just above the horizon.
A spark plug   a piston firing
over and over and over and over
I drive.
Hundreds of thousands of tiny explosions
propel me forward at inhuman speeds.

Freedom is four wheels and a full tank of gas.
I have measured out my freedom
tank by tank
town to town
state to state.

Roadside attractions   roadside distractions
America stashes her freaks on the side of the road.
Stop and see something weird in a jar.
Have a soda   a burger   and fries.
Chat with your waitress
whose friendly smile says "Come again"
but she already knows this is it
"Bye"
and   take off

A bouncy jog
a long distance call

a long drive on a lunatic golf range
a felt-tip pen switch fix
and the Eagle lifts off.
Buzz looks back.
Engine exhaust topples the stars and stripes.

SPINDLETOP
in memory of the first big oil well in Texas

Spindletop,
you're dry
a stripper operation
oil and gas
bump and grind
give it to me give it to me
pump it for the money.

When all that's left
is your sulphur face
and they take that too
leaving Spindletop trashed
a pockmarked wasteland.

Nobody cries for you
and nobody visits
It's easier to play a sentimental old tune
and look at pictures from the glory days
when you were pumping hard
a bona fide gusher.

APPLES

In these modern times, we
buy apples in boxes but a bite is too retro
for we modern kids, so we
hack into apples to take a taste
of what ought to be free.

WHITE PRIVILEGE

That's just how it is.
We live in the immovable center of the universe.
Now let's base science on false premise
in a world where the sun orbits the earth.

It's like that with White privilege,
if you're White.
There's no need to even talk about it.
Assume that White people are the center of the universe
and anyone who questions it
gets persecuted as a heretic.

Galileo is the best case scenario.
Life in prison,
then three hundred fifty years later
a public apology.

Who will build us a telescope
a microscope, maybe
to observe this absurdity?
Do we really have another two hundred years to equity?
Do we need revolution or evolution?
We know change has been so s l o w
like the earth around the sun.
And yet it moves.

PRECIOUS CHILD

Special snowflakes grow up to be nothing
but special cogs in a special machine.

Cry alligator tears and buy faux fur
organic monoculture bananas
organic shampoo   organic clothing.

Green like cash.   Paint every label green.
You can paint coal clean.
                                      Nuclear power
lets us dance all night like Carmen Miranda.

Now it's American dreams we're fracking.

Problems don't exist if they stay unseen.
We've bought everything green. We're proud owners
of the wasteland sinking like Atlantis.

Who will eat honey from the last beehive?
Who gets rich when the last elephant dies?

THE HATE U GIVE LITTLE INFANTS FUCKS EVERYBODY

Tupac is the new Jimi Hendrix.
You don't have to sell out anymore
cuz someone will do it for you when you're dead.

There don't seem to be any options left
so black and brown kids rebel
buying THUGLIFE t-shirts and notebooks and lunchkits.

They don't have a clue
that their money feeds the machine
that ground Tupac up
and spat his image out
onto t-shirts and notebooks and lunchkits
and these little infants who have been given hate
buy and buy and buy
and this also fucks everybody.

CRYBABY

Cassandra says
that every time she reads the news
she picks up a virus
and she says, *It's Stockholm Syndrome.*

She says, *It's not really worth it
to keep speaking the truth.*

She's had enough
of the rat race, *Like who really wants
to compete with rats anyway?* She says
she's never really found a bra that fits.

She says what's on her mind, but everybody thinks
she's skindiving the Sahara. She repeats herself,
The half life of a genius's regret is a thousand years. She says,
It's worse than we thought.

He says he really needs to take a break from this nuclear disaster.
She says, *Shut up. The people in Japan
don't get to take a break.*

Boo hoo. He says, *Boo hoo.
Nobody cares about your alligator tears.*

She fumbles for words. She gets flustered
from verbal attacks. She feels the fear of the conscientious.
She thinks of the teeth of a trap gripping a leg. She wonders
about what Demetrius and his brother did.

She says, *It's an urban legend.* She says, *It's a big lie.*
She says, *There's nothing to do if your country betrays you.*
It's a law, she says. She has so many headaches.
She can't sleep. She says, *There've been some problems.*

TOOLS

The half-hippy prince of San Francisco
has a kitchen table protocol
so I roll a joint for him.

He rants about the bitches of the aristocracy
barking orders
that hip-hop revolutions are bound to break.

People who have everything I ever wanted
make me think about all the things I never got
and don't miss now, so I tell him

The universe is most like a three-legged dog chasing its tail.

He bitches that when we use the tools of the elite
how can we expect anything but to be shackled by them?
Rules and forms and style and convention,
don't mention anything that might offend.
Write what you know
is a rule to follow
if what you know is edifying.
Otherwise
keep quiet about your life.

In a blaze of apathy, I give him a light.

THE JUNKY ELECTRIC

Instead of doing heroin
I'm reading Burroughs.
It's easier to navigate
a cut up landscape
than a series of electronic deadends
as I search for something once called
The News.

In our times
facts are determined
by a camera's angle.
The News
is no stranger
to government subsidies.

In our times
standard operating procedures
all used to be illegal.
That's corruption
a redefinition of ethical practice
that slices off its own nose.

But who am I to judge
and what can I do anyway.
I'm just another junky.   Got to feed
my need   for electricity
my nuclear fix
so I can read all night
and escape
in someone else's
altered state.

AMERICA GOES TO A FRAT PARTY

I have something to tell you
that you don't want to hear.

    He says *I love you* in Esperanto.

The music of our feelings
broadcasts on AM radio
on one scratchy speaker
in that old red Chevrolet.

Some people say
we're driving in the end times.
What do you think
Is it over?

    Oil spills and radiation are nothing new

But there's a frat party going on.
These big companies act like college kids
who got enough cash
to throw a keg party every night
And   you know   there's girls you marry
and girls you fuck.
America shows up every night
and she's leaned back over a folding chair.
She's got the keg tap in her mouth
gulping it down   gulping gulping it down.
Everybody's cheering her on.
The boys all laugh

    I wonder what else she'll swallow

She's gulping it down.
And if you've ever been to Spring Break

in Florida or Louisiana or Texas
you've seen her.   I've been her.
There's part of that fun
that's missing from my memory
until the part I'd rather forget
when beer turns to vomit.
I got my head in a toilet somewhere
and nobody's there to hold my hair.
America goes to this party every night
Can't stop won't stop gulping it down.

> *America the Beautiful*
> *I only got a quarter tank of gas left.*

So what do you think
Is it over?

> *There's too much static*
> *I can't hear the radio.*

MASS INCARCERATION

America reaches for delusional bootstraps
that slap back like a belt
whipping people of minimum wage.

America believes it's criminal to be crazy
in the land of the free samples
and the home of the brave soldiers
who trade their sanity
for false promises of the future
in the poverty draft.

America won't hire
veterans or felons
not even if you've served your time.

Mass incarceration
breeds a culture of alienation
and America's self-hatred
is inevitable recidivism.

For all the problems that she's caused them
America blames her children
and she solves them
like a vicious mother who eats her young.

CLIMATE CHANGE

This heat grips me
like the pleather embrace
of a discount dominatrix.

I like it.

You may call me perverse
but I like it
this new heat in Northern cities.

San Francisco's never been a frigid bitch
and she's always been for sale.
Her sweat stinks of sweet steam beer.
It's sometimes hard to navigate
her silicone valleys, her devil's slide.
But I cling to her commands

Flip that switch
Drive me, drive, drive

Her wish is my command.
I'm a willing slave
and everything I do
heats her up
sweat dribbling down
fishnets into stiletto boots.

DUMPSTER DIVE

Do you want to go dumpster dive the corner store?

In my mind's eye
I see ripe produce riddled with tiny spiral trails of radioactive isotopes.

I say
*I admire your urban survival skills
but you've been freaking out about plutonium all day
and now you want to rescue food
that's been overexposed.*

He says
*Well, I guess that's true.
At least we won't have to worry
about botulism or salmonella.*

THE ARCHIVE OF THE EVENING NEWS

The archive of the evening news
is the history of everything nobody cares about.

The boy in the well doesn't care
about the starving children in Africa
and he still won't eat his vegetables.

The starving children in Africa don't care
about gang violence in America
and they are still starving.

The little thugs already know that nobody cares
so they stay up late on a school night
and do things that children do
when nobody watches.   Film at eleven.

If a bad golf shot leads
the news
there's something going on
that we don't want to hear.

When forgettable footage of human interest closes
the news
I'm momentarily moved   a deep sentimentality
and tears.   I'm just as apt to cry
during holiday commercials
and the sappy parts of sci fi.

AMERICA DRIVES DRUNK

She's a bloated old whore
vomiting the Star-Spangled Banner
on the sidewalk.

O say
can you
Give it to me
Give it to me
I'm free

What happened?

I just wanna watch TV

Don't touch that dial!
We have remote control
vertical and horizontal hold.

We watch TV on endless stream
but there used to be a broadcast day.
They'd spin the Star-Spangled Banner
while we watched the astronauts
plant the flag on the moon.
The test pattern turned on
colored bars and blocks
and that single tone woke me up
if I fell asleep in front of the tube.

The happiest memories of my childhood
are of my family gathered.
My mother never cooked
so we watched TV together
Star Trek and Doctor Who
Wonder Woman and Saturday morning cartoons.

I liked the click of the dial.
I liked how static really looked like noise.
I liked to sit really close to the TV.
I didn't believe in radiation or god
or really anything I couldn't see.
My mother would scream
but I never did go blind.
I liked to press my eye against the curved glass.
I couldn't see inside
but I saw how the picture made itself
of millions of tiny boxes of color
constantly rearranging
to entertain us
to sustain us

What happened?

A crash
Drunk driver
As seen on TV

O say can you

Red   *eyes and blood*
White   *sidewalk, the ambulance*
Blue   *nitrile gloves*

Can you see?

PENT-UP RESPONSIBILITIES

Captain Amnesia can't remember why he wears red white and blue anymore. He isn't great with history or geography, and as far as politics go, a little hazy on presidents before and after Ford. He has a few stock phrases that roll off the tongue. I pledge allegiance to the flag of the United States of Amnesia! Frog Bless Amnesia! Amnesia the Beautiful! A halo of forgotten regrets rests heavier every day over his head. Damn. When did Just Wondering Woman start asking so many questions?

All our heroes look like puppets and clowns!
When did this happen? Where's the moral ground?
What happened to your memories? Listen!
Impotent hero! Great big chicken!
How many more drugs are there left to take?
Is drowning in vomit your boozy fate?
New motto: protect your stash, serve yourself.

Captain Amnesia listens infrequently, like a radio that fades in and out. The antennae are up, but nothing really comes through that well. Lately it's all been the same old song anyway.

Can you remember where you parked your car?
Why do I have to wear this stupid bra?

Captain Amnesia gets cranky when he doesn't know the answers. He wishes for the days when wars were simple and women might wonder, but they would never ask. He wishes that he could remember the name of his first grade teacher. She was really beautiful.

What about your job? What about your job?
Should I love you if you don't have a job?
Why do we fight? What are we fighting for?
What would happen if we stopped fighting wars?

He wishes he could remember the name of that war. But he can't. And worse, he is aware of the problems of Amnesia. He is aware of his woman's constant Socratic nagging. Yet his philosophy of action remains constant even in the face of critical questions and persistent doubts.

Tell me now
IS Amnesia BEAUTIFUL?

He can't remember what it's like to have a real moral struggle. And it doesn't help that the weather is changing. You can't predict much less be expected to remember the weather.

What time is it now?

I don't know.

If we end war, will we know how to act?
So aggressive by nature, by nurture
belligerent, blind, ignorant of peace,
how will we learn to live a peaceful life?
No living memory of peacetime days,
we have mutilated our tender youth,
generations of shellshocked veterans.
Would we know what to do if we just stop?
How would our economy work without war?
The war machine economy transforms!
My tax dollars fund schools and health care,
no more bombs or prosthetic devices.
I'm done funding a meatgrinder that eats
our own soldiers and little brown babies.

Send in the freakin clowns! Woman! Let me be! Please! Even if I could remember anything except a few vague feelings of attachment to you, I wouldn't want to! Every day! Can't you give me a break?

Do people in war zones
get to take breaks?

I can't even remember why it all started in the first place. Or what's going on now. So how can I be responsible? I can't. I'm not.

So, you recognize a bad decision
defend your bad action and continue
because that's the way it's always been done?

You don't understand. Unattentive citizens might be a blessing.

What?
What
do you mean?
Are we having the same conversation?

Maybe you should have some respect for your elders.

It's easy to ignore facts, isn't it?
More bad things happen
when heroes just quit
doing hero jobs.
Aren't you worried about the future?

I stopped worrying about the future.

That's because you can't remember the past.
Not anything.
At all.
Ever.
Can you?

Captain Amnesia is quiet. All he can remember is the last time their bellybuttons touched. But he can't remember exactly when that was. He is breathing in out in out in out watching his belly, thinking of the night and of the bedsheets winding around them, around their legs. Their faces pressed together. Words. No words.

Did you hear? Did you hear about that crash?

No.

A drunk driver. Drunk driving has to stop.

You have to stick to it.

Weren't you even listening to me?
Did you hear what I said to you at all?

You should mind your own business.

I'm Just Wondering, what makes me love you?
What makes me run after heroes like you?
Are you really ready to go the way
of flared jeans, newspapers, and dodo birds?
Are you going to curl up in a ball
alone in your climate-controlled bunker
and smugly ponder the fact that you will
starve slower than your neighbors and their kids?

Captain Amnesia gets up and leaves again. Maybe he can tolerate so much nagging because he has no capacity to remember any of her questions. He prefers the company of strangers. So he walks out on her again. He can't remember how many times she's taken him back. He has uncomfortable feelings, but he can't quite put his finger on those either. He quells an audible whimper. His deferred regrets have begun to demand payment.

He usually prefers to drive, but he walks to the bar. He spends his two dollar bill collection on beer, and he doesn't even get that drunk. Damn. Thomas Jefferson confuses him anyway, and he's not really sure whose idea it was to mint a two dollar bill in the first place.

He hops on the bus. He watches a boy in a hoodie put his arm around a girl in a tight skirt. The city bus is the municipal confessional. Strangers confess, and he listens to talk about a boy who was murdered and a magic bra that fits. He hears the hiss of the brakes. He steps down and like magic the back doors of the bus open.

He walks. Accusations that he is a sociopath always surprise him. He knows that Cassandra Syndrome is real, and he knows that Amnesians will never know the truth. He has moments of guilt, but he forgets them so easily. He is easily distracted, and he has plenty of money. There's a question mark stitched over his heart.

ONE SUPERHERO WON'T BE ENOUGH

We don't really understand cause and effect.
We are a nation of villains
unaware of our villainy.

We ordinary villains
let our dogs shit anyplace they please.
Our prescient pooches already know
where destiny will put each foot.

We leave a trail of trash
like birdcrumbs never to be followed back.

We leave the lights on
let the water run while we brush our teeth.

We can't imagine what life would be like
without central air and heat.

We have no idea where our food comes from
or where each flush goes.

We're morally outraged at the suggestion of sorting trash
Can't we just buy different products in greener packages?
Can't we just pay somebody cash to help keep America looking good?

Isn't that enough?

You're a dirty little girl

He says to me in Esperanto.
He feels most comfortable expressing himself
in Klingon
or Esperanto
So it's possible that's an attempt at flirting.

I still don't have superpowers
He complains
I walk unprotected
through clouds of radiation.
All my favorite foods have genetic modifications.
I've been bitten by spiders
and stepped in psychic dog shit.
I am an American
so it's probably for the best
I still don't have superpowers.
I like to think that I'd use my powers for good
but I'd just end up selling
laundry detergent
or garbage bags
kitchen gadgets
or fast food.

What about you? What would you do
if the myths came true
and it was   you
who stepped straight out of a comic frame?
How many of us ordinary villains
would struggle into extraordinary tights
and remember to turn out the lights
before running off to save another day?

ACKNOWLEDGEMENTS

Grateful acknowledgement is given to the editors of the publications which previously published my poems:

The 16th & Mission Review: Drive (2007), Bombed (2008)
Dark Matter: A Journal of Speculative Writing: Apples (2012)
Dead Flowers: A Poetry Rag: Dumpster Dive (2012)
Haight Ashbury Literary Journal: Telecommunications (2013)
Meniscus: Proselytize (2017)
Nerve Cowboy: Dating Poets (2012)
Out of Our: My Navel is a Funhouse Mirror (2013)
phati'tude Literary Magazine: ¿What's in a Nombre? Writing Latin@ Identity in America: I Learned All My Spanish in School (2012)
River, Blood, and Corn: Mythic Arcade (2016), Siblings (2016), I Learned All My Spanish in School (2016)
Soul Vomit: Beating Domestic Violence: Advice (2012)
Sparring with Beatnik Ghosts Anthology: One Superhero Won't Be Enough (2011)
Sweet Wolverine: A Collection: Precious Child (2015)

I deeply appreciate the open mic poetry hosts of the San Francisco Bay Area who create the spaces that welcome all poets to share their poems. Many thanks also to the poets who participate—from the cranky to the sublime.

It has been an amazing experience to work with an editor, and one who has helped me set new goals for my writing. Thank you for helping me make my poetry as widely accessible as literacy will allow, Natasha Dennerstein.

I am grateful for the many encouragements from friends, family, teachers, students, and all the librarians in my life. Extra special thanks to Parry who hears every poem every time.

E. K. KEITH is a Latinx poet who calls San Francisco home, but her hometown is Houston where she learned to write in the sprawl. She performs her poems on the street corner and takes the mic at coffee shops, bars, and radio stations. Her work appears online and in magazines on all three coasts and places beyond, and *Ordinary Villains* is her first book of poetry. E.K. organizes Poems Under the Dome, San Francisco's annual open mic celebration of Poetry Month inside City Hall. Her work as a public school librarian creates opportunities for her to make the world a better place every day.